Her Northern Star

Priyanka

BookLeaf Publishing

India | USA | UK

Presentation by *BookLeaf Publishing*

Web: www.bookleafpub.com

E-mail: info@bookleafpub.com

ISBN: 9789360941789

First edition 2024

Dedicated to the Universe.

ACKNOWLEDGEMENT

I would like to express my immense gratitude to the universe for aligning synchronicities in my life so that I could be aware that there exists a deeper essence to life, and that I am forever embraced by its watchful care.

PREFACE

At the heart of this collection lies a tale of mistaken identity, wherein the author once mistook the brightest star in the evening sky as a Northern Star. Later in her life, despite realising her error, she found solace in the belief that the first and brightest star she saw in the evening was her own Northern Star, her own beacon of hope guiding her through life's uncertainties. "My Northern Star" invites readers on a journey of introspection and discovery, encouraging them to find their own guiding light amidst the darkness and to never cease wishing upon stars.

The Clouds and Her

Whenever her eyes were full of tears,
Up above, clouds conspired.
Coming in all shapes and sizes,
Sometimes her imagination playing up
Or it must have been her knight....
Who knows...clouds conspired for her to smile.

This connection goes wayyyyy back!!
When she was naive amongst matures,
Fighting her tears when she used to run and hide.
Sometimes under her safe shelter made of that umbrella covered with sheets,

Right there sitting with a bowl of maggi, she used to weep.

And often she used to hear that whooshing sound of the breeze,
That was an indication to run up to those railings...
Beyond which there was a smokey clouds' trail.
Looking above, she revered those clouds...
As they used to envelop her in warmth when she was alone in the crowd.

Crowd of predators, each of their own species...
Not refraining to spare her heart no matter what she did for averting their crisis.
Now when the sky gets dark, it soothes her soul,
Cause why should she be afraid, when she has her clouds.

Clouds and her?? Well, synchronicities are way too many to just be called synchronicities.
Now she knows when her eyes will well up, it will just be momentary.
Clouds will soon conspire to rain over her tapestry.
So she is calm, looking above with immense gratitude in her heart, free of pain.

Understanding life in ways where even maturity fails.
Clouds have all along been her Knight!...
Who would have thought she befriended the Universe when predators were befriending their prey...
That must be the reason she is 'alive', free from their trap of lies.

Wearing her heart on her sleeves, knowing when her eyes will weep,
Her clouds will rain, washing away all her worldly pain.

The Celestial Sapien

In every fleeting moment, the moon pines for
her grace,
In the dark night, it yearns for just one glimpse
of her face.
As she gazes at the sky, her hands clasped tight,
Whispers of "so beautiful," fill the tranquil
night.

"Her moon", once a distant orb in space,
Now, an emblem of her singular embrace.
Her faith, a force that moves mountains,

Worked for her to be in her moon's silver haze.

The stubbornness of her heart won over the moon.
The moon, captivated, in her love,
Now, too wished to be hers.
Time stretches on, each night an eternity,
Yearning for the moment, their celestial unity.

The moon longed to reach its zenith high.
To be in her presence, to control her emotional tides.
To tell her that she can have, every star and the sun,
For she, the Celestial Sapien is the chosen one.

That Sacred Name

Sometimes someone's name becomes so sacred,
She wonders who else has experienced this dilemma,
Of whether you just love a name or love a name because it's the name of the person you love.

She wonders what he will do if he knows the extent of her feelings,
And how insanely she has harboured them.

But she often wonders, does he have an inkling
of what she is going through?
How can he not possibly know when every other
hour of the day,
With every breath she takes, she doesn't forget to
take his name.
His name has become as sacred as that of a
revered faith.

He will run far away if he finds out;
It's not that he is, at this moment, very close...
But after knowing the depth of her feelings,
He will be overwhelmed,
And she, again, will be abandoned...
So why would she ever tell him?

But sometimes she wishes to tell him that he can
be this meaningful to someone...
That he can be the person someone would wish
for while talking to the moon and stars,
That every evening and night someone can wait
for the moon and stars to rise...
Only to make a childlike wish upon them and
patiently wait for the Universe to answer back in
some way.

That he is worthy of this kind of sacred
romance,
in which the entire cosmos is playing a role,

And unfortunately, he is the villain, playing with her heart's chords.
If he only knew how much she felt for him.

What melancholy it is that he will never know there was a girl who waited for him,
In darkness and in light,
she thought about him day and night.
That he was her gravity,
giving her hope when everything was lost.
That he both gained and lost her of all social calculation.
Once there was a girl who felt for him like no other.
No, he will never know.
He is that unfulfilled wish that she has decided to let go.

Grey Roses

She found a place she thought was home,
When she stepped in, the cruel reality crashed down.
What seemed like a bed of roses, sweet and bright,
Turned out to be thorns, hidden from sight.

They pricked her hands, bloodied her soul.
Her self-respect, which she has crushed herself,
Again and again, like a self-imposed storm,
Waited to be quelled.

How to overcome, how to heal?
She asked the divinity, begging on her knees.
Seeking to be in the embrace of her creator,
Where she can be cured.

The red petals she admired have turned grey,
In the hope of the unknown, roses were kept.
But now she holds the bouquet of thorns
As a reminder of an endless ache,
Which time will surely heal, if not her faith.

An Unending Quest

Let's find those words that can be said when you can't express the extent of your feelings,
For those times when you are rendered speechless with all those little things.

For someone who has no precise excuse to be there,
But still, that person selflessly chooses to be near.

For calming your erratic heart and making time
for you,
Where a few minutes easily change into long
hours.
Funnily though it's not enough even then.

You might wonder when it happened...
At what moment your conscious mind made a
decision,
That person you are talking to is not just an
illusion.
Where exactly you crossed that threshold?
When exactly your emotions multiplied
tenfold?!

Don't lie to yourself; you have read and re-read
your conversations...
Hell, yes!! You sure are keeping lots of
expectations.
Though we both know expectations never meet
reality,
The situation that you are in will never have
clarity...

So why do you wonder if you have crossed his
mind once?
You already are aware it's not always the same
for everyone!
Why are you choosing to be so vocal??

Let it go; you already know how it is to be
special...
Let his generosity be acknowledged by your
heart;
Don't you mess up the natural schedule of being
apart.

So why don't you forget your quest to find those
words,
Sure enough it's not in the world's lexicon,
And you know you won't find it until you know
for sure that's what your heart wants...

Maybe for better or worse even some voids are
meant to be,
This is the only understanding that you should
have to get rid of this agony.

Love the void, love the pure connection;
Everything in this world is not supposed to be
the epitome of perfection,
So why are you keen on asking so many
questions?
Just let it be, let it go...
your quest does not have an ending
That much you should definitely know.

The Closure

What was that feeling, she wondered
The thin line for her, for a second, got blurred.
So she ran away unable to confront
or it would have made her the hypocrite of the
season.
The unrequited nothingness often leads to
permanent scars,
But she wondered, what was that feeling??

If only she was the reckless one,
Not caring about the outcome.

Maybe then she would have dared to talk her
heart out,
To give a closure to something which never even
had its beginning.

She wondered how did this happen, at what
moment her heart became so fragile?
Going out of her way just to make sure
everything is okay,
Looking everywhere till her eyes reach there,
Finding comfort in that awareness of those
nanoseconds,
She wonders if she is the only one with these
whirlpools of emotions.

Then she reminds herself she has a far-fetched
role to pretend.
But then to what end?
When it's completely one-sided and others will
portray themselves as nothing less than a victim.

A step to and fro, to and fro....
The fear for her was tangible though.
Increased heartbeat, that unable to breathe kind
of feeling.
The fear to do something undeniably wrong...
Not for herself but for others involved as well.
Though in a matter of few minutes, she realised,
It was just her, again she being the naive herself.

Thinking the world is either white or black,
forgetting people often are just classic grey.
All people care about is themselves,
their well-being, their life, their stories,
and in the process of gaining this
self-satisfaction they make others as their
collateral.

How cruel is this phenomenon, she wondered.
Why do people make people care about them,
when they can't do that in the first place?
Why it's always for selfish reasons, why people
can't just appreciate people as a person.
Then she forgets she is not just a person,
with dozens of titles attached,
she hardly can be perceived as a human with
emotions.

The guilt of feeling the unknown seems like the
ultimate betrayal of broken principles.
How forgiveness for this can be achieved, she
wondered,
Maybe this self-disgust must be punishment
enough.
This terrible feeling is the polar opposite of that
unknown one.
But she wondered, what was that feeling?

Treading on the path that leads only to disaster,
She denies to walk any further,
Hence she chose to close her eyes to not let her heart be compromised.
Firmly she decides to take an oath to not even wonder what was that feeling.
Letting go of all that happened inside her heart and mind,
For her, this is a closure, one of its own kind.

The Meadow of Dreams

In a backyard bathed in golden light,
She lingered, lost in tales of flight.
No Edward, Bella, in the meadow's gleam,
Just harsh reality, devoid of dream.

Why, she pondered, in this world so cold,
Does imagination's warmth not take hold?
Analysing, searching, she found no reply,
For this practical world made her dreams defy.

In the woods, she sat, thoughts a-swirl,
But reality's grasp made her world unfurl.
Transition looming, pain on the rise,
As she's asked to shed her dreamy guise.

Her mind, a canvas of fiction's play,
Where "unconditional" holds sway.
But in this world, where loss is real,
She must let go.

Shattered, yet she'll find her way,
Through this transition, come what may.
For in the depths of her soul's terrain,
A survivor's spirit, she'll maintain.

Unwinding Verses

Don't read, dear reader, this verse is mine to keep,
For my mind's restless waves, I seek solace deep.
To rewind, delete memories that pain and sting,
Triggers of feelings, unnecessary they bring.

Whom to blame but myself, for allowing those mistreatment?
In the depths of my thoughts, no zenith, no retreat.

Yet amidst imagined realms, a fleeting calm I find,
As if the journey's end soothes the restless mind.

How did he hold my heart's string, amidst the storm's roar?
Becoming my polar star, on turbulent seas I adore.
Unaware of the pain he caused, remnants still remain,
In crowds I seek him, but find only vague disdain.

No longer do I crave, I've let go of the past,
Irresponsible and lame.
Yet in darkness, the urge to share my daily plight,
multiplies tenfold, longing for the light.

The Revelations

As the purple petals fade to blue,
Life reveals what's worth holding true.
It changed deceiving perceptions,
The selfless ego started questioning others'
intentions.
And that's how emotional maturity knocked her
over,
Wiping her lens and finally showing true
colours.

Beneath illusions, lies the art,
Of connections true, that soothe the heart.
In shadows deep, and light's reflection,
She finds the beauty, in every deception.

Falling from the Pedestal

She often finds herself adrift in pensive realms,
Contemplating   myriad   what-ifs   and   unseen
helms.
Yet how does she elude the stark verity,
That she's shed the pristine cloak of her purity?

Once, she adorned the pedestal of pristine grace,
In thought and deed, an ideal's embrace.
But love's immutable hold led her to falter,
And from her lofty perch, she was cast asunder.

Now, remorse, a spectre, haunts her path,
Its silent whispers, an ever-present wrath.
In this taboo domain, close to her embrace,
Can she find solace, or must she simply efface?

Yet in the depths of her subconscious realm,
Where dreams unfurl and memories overwhelm,
She is the protagonist, enacting her crime,
A recurring motif in the theatre of time.

Perhaps redemption lies in baring her soul,
In confessing the anguish that takes its toll.
To seek forgiveness, not from external source,
But from within, to mend her spirit's course.

The Strength Within

In endless nights, my mind has sought,
One memory, a beacon, bravely brought,
To battle shadows of childhood past,
And fill the voids that forever last.

Given one chance to reverse the flow,
Escape the darkness where I once did grow,
Yet, heartfelt moments evade my grasp,
Leaving me adrift in the endless expanse.

But perhaps therein lies the key,
To who I am, what I've come to be,
For in the absence of light, I've found,
A strength within, unbound, unbound.

Pursuit of Simplicity

If only contentment were in materialistic things of life,
It would have been far too easy.
Which is why we are apt with the whirlpool of temporary emotions and some permanent feelings...
Only peace was in the pomp and show of happening life, it would have been far too easy.
That's why we are met with some irrevocable equations and some undecipherable heartache...
If only little things didn't mean too much.

Who is going to listen?

Getting pro at constant pretence where everything is okay and fine.
Making them believe those smiles are genuine.
Anyway, who is going to care about sleepless nights?
About a ruthless fight with one's own mind?
The urge to talk to someone, the urge to be cared for emotionally...
That wish of being that person, not to be given up so easily.
For reciprocation of the tendency to hold on for infinity...
Again, who is going to listen to these endless thoughts of nights?
Someday, maybe someone will ask, "What's wrong?"

And the answer to that question will matter for
real.
The concern won't be temporary;
it just won't be to start and end the conversation.
It will have soulful meaning and purpose.

And then further the mind wonders at 3:45
Whether these thoughts of hope and light are
even worth the unfair fight?
Isn't the outcome already known?
In this materialistic and practical world,
emotions are not something that people hold on
to for long.
That's apparently how we become "mature" and
"strong."
By giving up what we believe in the most.
All the conspiracies and agendas of others will
tire you out,
to keep fighting for what's right.
You will burn in the end, and the people you will
burn for won't even look twice.

That's how the world works, no?
Forgetting the good, remembering the bad.
How is our species surviving all this nonsensical
stress?
The questions are endless, but again, the
question is: who is going to listen?

Endless Questions

Endless questions swirling in her mind...
Giving her exhaustive sleepless nights.
Hiding under her blanket, don't want to wake up
just for people's sake
For once, can she be selfish??

All she wants is to escape to a place where her
existence will synchronise with her essence.
Where there will be no boundaries or
regulations.
Where she will be she without any
consideration.

But who is she? Again, is the same question.
Can't anyone just care for her once?
In her mind, everything is about reciprocation.
Then why her care is not reciprocated?

Why are people slyly double-faced?

How to be optimistic when surrounded by negativity?
Why do people conspire to pull others down when they have the power and opportunity?
Why can't power be translated into something good?

Tired of the constant strife,
She seeks solace in the silent night,
Hoping for peace, yearning for light.

Body and Soul

The lost soul, which was hiding in a hole,
Was finally found by a body completely pure.

What made the soul lost?
Only happiness is what it would have cost.

But still, deep within, the soul was scarred;
Not even an iota of love was on the cards.

Feeling lost, it wandered around
Until it was fascinatingly found.

The body thought the soul was pure.
What it didn't know is that there is no cure.

The poison of darkness still takes hold;
Never has it been thought to take a step so bold.

In a dilemma of strength and weakness,
The soul forgot to heal itself.

Now the consequence lies ahead;
Losing the body is what the soul is afraid of.

Pain and happiness are something that walk
along.
Now the soul wishes it hadn't been found.

Moments of joy can't be counted
single-handedly
When pain so deep is outright deadly.

Still, how could the soul leave the body alone?
It is fate that has decided to intertwine them as
one.

Body and soul shall always stay together
Unless fate decides to take away the soul
forever.

The Prime Façade

Then there are people surrounded by people,
Thinking they have got it all...
It's a prime façade put up by people
Who are desperately waiting for their great fall.

Beware, my friend, beware!!
From such people who are the sweet poison,
Meant to be in your life to teach you a lesson.

The lesson of finding true people close to your
heart,
To keep them there and never be apart.
To not throw them off 'cause of your illicit
affair,
Remember, they might be few but
Those are the people who actually care.
Beware, my friend, beware!!

The Sweet Chorus

In darkness' hold, she heard, "You could never!"
Jolted back to consciousness, shivering, she
woke up through night's endeavour.
Wrapped in darkness, she clutched her quilt
tight,
Finding comfort in the glimmer coming from the
small window high.

Gazing at the sky's bright hue,
Tracing dawn's ascent, as it painted anew.
Hearing birds chirping so pure and free,
She wondered, do they wait through the night
for their morning spree?

Their twitter and their chirps, a language sweet and clear,
From night's deep slumber, they readily appear.
Yet there she lay, hesitant to rise,
Wishing for the freedom found in morning skies.

Embracing the Paradox

Being a witness to life's ever-turning tide,
Moments of joy and sorrow side by side,
Tears and laughter entwined, emotions run deep,
In the rhythm of life's dance, we sway and weep.

Amidst the laughter, echoes of pain,
In the depths of sorrow, glimpses of gain,
Connected by threads of shared humanity,
In every tear shed, lies a story of unity.

And as we stand on the shores of time,
Watching the world's symphony intertwine,
We embrace the paradox, the bittersweet blend,
For in life's weave, every thread finds its end.

Echoes of Redemption

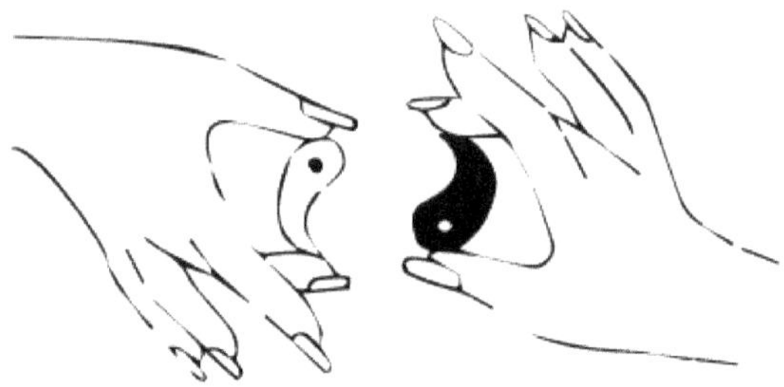

In the gentle grasp of empathy's embrace,
Where we seek perfection in the quiet of night's
space,
Let go of guilt's relentless chase,
Welcome the light, let shadows find their place.

Value the moments, be grateful and kind,
Recognize efforts with a humble mind,
Avoid impulsive urges, their tempting song,
Past actions, once rejected, may still belong.

In the world's judgement, stark and clear,
No nuances, just black and white appear,
Yet within yourself, seek truth's gentle light,
In impulsive moments, take flight.

No grand plan, no fate's decree,
Just you, grappling with thoughts silently,
Seek forgiveness with a quiet plea,
Find amnesty in your own reflection's decree.

Acceptance whispers on the breeze,
Letting go, under the moon's soft ease,
For those who are absent, let memories cease,
In clarity's embrace, find inner peace.

Don't deceive yourself, stand in truth's embrace,
Hold wisdom close, and walk with grace,
In the dance of poetry, amidst life's song,
Embrace the journey, where you truly belong.

Seeking Escape

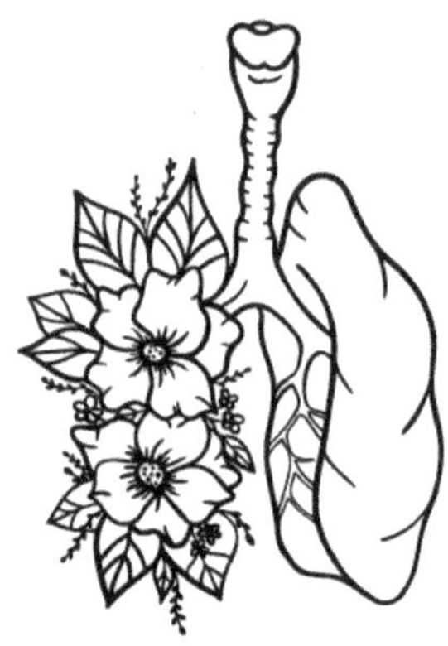

Within this darkness our soul chooses to survive,
Sometimes to revive what has been lost,
To respect what has been left...
I often wonder whether this is what the heart
only cares about.

The whole mathematics of life is in front of the
eyes,
Waiting to be resolved, to be ambushed...
I wonder if this is something that should be
sought.

Eyes weep when life multiplies pain,
Brain struggles to keep the heart sane,
Why this all is caused who knows,
I just often wonder, isn't there any way out?

A Beautiful Deception

And here we go again with so many blurred
notions...
And now left wondering how it's been such a
beautiful deception,
To find that niche where everything is white and
no grey...
Cause grey is WRONG.
It deceives, it shatters... worse than black.
It's a facade that will leave you in shackles.
Shackles of those endless thoughts,
of what-ifs and what-nots,
Of that never-ending ache, where your sanity is
at stake.